JOB INTERVIEW ESSENTIALS

NEIL O'DONNELL

For Mom and Dad, the sweetest and kindest individuals I ever met.

FOREWORD

Having worked with clients on six of seven continents, it seems only fitting that this Buffalo-born Irishman write this book in Germany while on a pseudo-vacation visiting family and friends and providing career guidance to millennials and Gen-Zers. As for the seventh continent, Antarctica, I'm still working on that.

I am a nationally certified, professional career coach who has worked with established professionals, new graduates, and jobseekers seeking management positions in their field or individuals seeking to enter new fields all together. I have published extensively on career-related topics including résumé writing, cover letter writing, and conducting job searches.

This book builds on earlier, award-winning guides I wrote providing career advice for jobseekers. Whereas my previous writings looked at resumes and cover letters, here I wanted to tackle the craft of job interviewing. Frankly, it's an art of sorts, performing for an audience, portraying the role of a successful employee when you've never worked for the employer. That is what you are essentially doing. In an interview, a good job interviewer will put you to task and see how you would address given situations. Likewise, a good interviewer will take stock of how you carry yourself with others. If you represent yourself poorly before, during, and immediately after the interview, that will say a lot about how you would represent the employer should they hire you.

Fair or not, these are the concerns interviewers have and will explore during the interview. So, preparing to excel during any interview is crucial. Think of an interview as a performance, for in many respects IT IS! Yes, those of us with acting backgrounds have a slight advantage here. Now, per my mother and father's regulations, you should always treat others with respect and decency; be compassionate and understanding to even those who disrespect you. I am assuming everyone always follows my parent's rules. That said, I have battled anxiety my entire life, specifically a severe case of Obsessive-compulsive Disorder. For me and many others, being gregarious in unfamiliar AND familiar settings is difficult to say the least. Yet, in an interview, you must be outgoing and introduce yourself to interviewers and other staff you encounter, because you never know whose feed-back a would-be employer will consider regarding your candidacy.

Yeah, those secretaries that a job interviewee shrugged off and was cold to? Interviewers often ask these professionals how job candidates treated them.

In interviews, I am a mess, to be honest. Yet, for all interviews I practice my performance, which is what makes a huge differ-ence! This book is geared toward helping you prepare for your interview performance. If, like me, you have a medical condition that makes it difficult to speak or otherwise 'perform' in public settings, that issue is taken into account here. The reality is that rarely does someone get hired because of the résumé and/or cover letter she or he submitted. Those documents are more for landing a job interview. Consequently, the interview performance is key to prep for, and for those with severe anxiety, you must practice in handling that anxiety. As a side note, I urge anyone with medical conditions and/or battling anxiety to reach out to a therapist for assistance. This book in no way can take the place of a trained medical practitioner. I waited until I was 35 before I sought help, and the help I received has made life better and my anxiety much more manageable. Please ask for help, because there is no shame in getting assistance when needed. Trust me! We all need assistance from time to time. Actually, a lot of advice contained herein was given to me by my parents and mentors. I`m just passing the advice on.

Now, what about my success rate? Outside of freelance writing where I bid on jobs, I have applied for eight jobs over the last 25 years. I successfully secured seven of those eight jobs, and I received very positive feedback on how I interviewed from five of those seven employers. My first couple jobs I never really sought feedback, so I can't give specifics on how I fared in those interviews. I got the job, though, and both of those employers have served as references for me in future job searches; I think that speaks volumes. As for my clients, I can`t conceive of a method for calculating rates of success, because I present at conferences and lecture for classes on interviewing skills contin-ually. I have no idea the ultimate number of those who have heard my advice. As for those who worked one-on-one with me to prepare for a job interview, more than 90% have obtained the job or a second interview after our working together. Of course, these stats lack knowledge of how poorly or well others (my clients' competition) interviewed for the same job. Be that as it may, readers can check out reviews of my work on Upwork.com to see what my clients have said about my assistance.

So, moving forward, think of the interview as your opportunity to show how great an employee you could be in the role you are applying for. Are you ready?

SET APPOINTMENT AND PREP TIME

You've sent in your résumé and cover letter, waiting a torturous amount of time to hear back, and learning that you indeed have been granted an interview for your dream job. Congratulations! Now what?

Well, you got a couple things that you have to do right away. First, you have to call and select an interview time. Seriously, I'm not even going to attempt to separate the different camps regarding what is the best time to select. In some cases, an employer doesn't give you a choice. What happens is that the hiring manager or hiring committee sets a time for you and you have no choice but to take the time. Usually, however, you (the interviewee) are given a couple choices of times with which to meet with the hiring manager or hiring committee. If given a choice, I select the morning hour on the first day of interviews. Why? I'm alert in the mornings, whereas in the afternoons I start to lose a lot of energy, and I select the first day partially because I want to get the thing over with (I have some anxiety issues, and waiting for a later interview date would cause me stress I don't need). I have heard different opinions from different 'career experts' regarding what is the appropriate time to select. Some career professionals argue that it is important to take one of the earlier interview slots so that you can make an impression, and those who interview after you will have to live up to your standard. On the other side of the coin, there are career professionals that argue you should select the last or one of the last interview slots to make certain your impact on the hiring manager or hiring committee is fresh in their minds.

Seriously, it's a mixed bag when it comes to the habits and preferences of hiring managers and hiring committees. For that reason, I encourage my clients to select the time that feels good. If you struggle early in the mornings, don't select an interview time that's early in the morning. If, like me, your energy drops off significantly after two or 3 o'clock, choose an earlier interview time. This comes down to you making a decision that is best for your performance. Yes, this is a performance; you are trying to show them the best that you will bring to the job, which is why it's important to select an interview time suited to your preferences.

Now, before we go on, there's a couple things I need you to do, or rather questions you need to ask when setting up your interview time. First, ask who will be interviewing you. If it's more than one person, try to get the names or at least the position titles of the individuals who will be interviewing you. In the event that the person you contact to set up your interview will not release the names of the interviewers, asking the titles of those individuals may help you narrow down the search and determine who it is that will be asking you questions. The second thing you need to do is ask how much time you will be allotted and if there will be more than one group interviewing you. In some cases, interviewees will have as many as three interviews: one with a hiring committee, one with the office staff, and one with the director or senior manager. We'll discuss all of this and its importance in a little bit.

Travel Costs

If the job you have applied for is a great distance away, traveling there may require you to rent a car, take a bus, or take an airplane (not to mention meals and a hotel room). If you will be incurring such travel costs, especially air travel and a hotel stay, it might be worth it to ask if travel expenses will be paid. From my experience, C-level positions at companies (CEO. CFO, etc.) often pay for a candidate's travel expenses. Many other industries do not (though I was pleasantly surprised when learning that many small companies and institutions do cover some or all travel costs). I would simply ask whether expenses were covered, and if you are informed no, you will have to decide whether or not it is an expense you can afford. If you are really strapped for cash but really interested in the position, request a phone interview or an interview be done using Skype or similar technology. More and more businesses are looking to videoconferencing for conducting interviews. As a note to any hiring managers or search committee members reading this, please don't be a jerk and hold it against a job candidate for inquiring about whether or not travel expenses are covered. Travel is a huge expense to manage during a job search, especially if a candidate is unemployed. I believe a candidate is well within her/his rights to inquire about travel expenses. That said, for candidates, if travel expenses are not covered, don't be a jerk about it. Companies often have little room in the budget for such expenses, especially small businesses. If you apply to a job out of state, be mindful that you may need to pay all costs to travel to attend an interview.

Preparation Time

Once you've selected your interview time, you need to look towards your own schedule with regards to preparing for that interview. As I have mentioned in previous books, you need to treat your job search as a full-time job. Likewise, you need to prep for your job interview, treating the prep time as your job (a job that essentially is replacing the 'job search' job). Now, in some cases you may only have a matter of one or two days before the interview. In other instances, you may have up to two weeks to prepare for a job interview, which is quite common for more advanced positions. Why the delay in being interviewed? For businesses, there is a significant component of planning and schedule-changing to accommodate for the hiring process, which includes interviewing prospective candidates. This is especially true when a hiring committee is involved. With a hiring commit-tee, the company needs to select interview times that correspond to openings in the hiring committee members' schedules. In the event that one of the candidates is from out of town, the hiring committee may also need to make arrangements for travel (some companies will pay for travel expenses for a candidate, but it takes time to make those arrangements). There are other logistics that need to be worked out such as arranging for parking passes or other clearances for interviewees, but I think you get the gist.

Regardless of the time you have in which to prepare for an inter-view, whether two days or two weeks, you have to schedule prep time. Some people will just wing it, putting in no prep time and just showing up for the interview. For these individuals, I don't think this strategy works out as well as they think it does. True, there are some that pull it off and do well in interviews with no prep, but those individuals in my experience are few and far between. Prep time is essential for getting yourself set and prepared with the right knowledge with which to prove to your potential new employer that you are the absolute best candidate from the pool of interviewees. There are four things you definitely need to set time aside for in preparation for your interview:

1. **Research the company and/or the department you are applying to work for.**
2. **Research the job/position you are applying for (yes, you should have done this already, but now is the time to make certain you know the ins and outs of the position as much as possible).**
3. **Research the individuals interviewing you.**
4. **Schedule breaks throughout the day.** As a stress management professional, I can tell you that clients going through preparation for interviews find themselves under immense stress. For this reason, I implore you to make certain that each day, while preparing for the interview, you make certain to have some down time. True, this will be a wee bit difficult if you're working another job, but it is nevertheless crucial that you set aside time for just you to relax. For me, hiking in the woods, reading fantasy and sci-fi novels, and writing are great releases. Okay, playing Warcraft also helps me to relax. You want to find activities that will help you get your mind off of the job interview and interview preparation. If you don't, you are not going to be well rested when you show up for your interview, which is something that will likely hurt your performance.
5. **Do a test drive to get to the interview site.** I am going to mention this a couple times. It is critical that you arrive 15 to 20 minutes early to the interview. One of the best ways to assure that this happens is to make certain you know how to get to the place where they

will interview you. Admittedly I probably take this to an extreme in that I run two, three, or four test drives to get to the interview location. I try and drive the route at the precise time I would be doing it on the day of the interview to gauge traffic flow. I also make a habit of looking for parking options prior to the day of the interview, because you do not want to be late, even after doing two or three test drives, because you couldn't find a parking space. As for the day of the interview, I recommend you time it so you arrive and are in a parking space 45 minutes before the interview. Then, you can take 10 to 15 minutes to relax, do some breathing exercises, and/or go over any important information you want to share in the interview. Listen, I know this sounds corny, but I for one can't stand it when an interviewee is late for an interview. Worse, there are employers who will totally rule out candidate if he or she arrives late, especially if the job opening was due to the previous person in that position being fired for always being late.

2

DO YOUR RESEARCH

You're still here? Very cool! Okay, you have the interview date set and you have a plan of action in place. Now what? I'm glad you asked. The name of the game at this point is research. Remember all those research papers you did in high school and college? Here's where all those late nights doing papers last-minute pays off. As I stated earlier, you won't likely have an entire semester-length of time in which to prepare for an interview, and in some cases you will only have one or two days to prepare. You're going to be cramming a lot of research into a short window of time. Now, there are a lot of people who seem to skip this part. I am amazed, beyond amazed, at how many interviewees clearly did next to no research! These individuals stand out like the proverbial sore thumb. In other words, they look really, really bad. I mean, they truly give a poor impression to interviewers, whether it's a hiring manager or hiring committee interviewing the job applicant.

Let me just take a second here to reiterate this point, because a lot of poor interviews simply come down to the fact that an interviewee did no research. You could be the greatest person in the world for the job you're applying to, but you need to show that in an interview to truly have a chance to get the job. Many less-qualified applicants get jobs simply because the better candidate did horribly in the interview, and the poor performance is generally tied to poor research preparation. Don't make this mistake!

Research the Company

Later in this book I will provide a list of questions that generally come up in interviews. Let me give you a preview of those questions right now. Any good interviewer is going to seek to assess your knowledge of the company. I am still perplexed by the large number of interviewees that, when asked what they know about the company, who revert to the 'deer in headlights' look. Now, for those who have done this, you are not alone. From my experience, 25% to maybe 50% of interviewees give that same look because they didn't do their research. As hiring managers and hiring committees will seek to eliminate poor candidates through the interview process, lack of knowledge about the company is a great way to rule someone out. So, in other words, research the company! The more you know, the better off you are. Granted, as we have already discussed, you may only have a matter of days in which to conduct this research before the interview. So, focusing your research efforts will be key to your success. Below are some of the major things I recommend jobseekers research about companies. Before going over that list, however, I want to stress one thing. When applying for jobs, it will help you tremendously if you start researching the company before you even apply for a job. First, this research will help you determine if the company is an entity you actually want to be employed by. I think it's fair to say that an individual who is a vegan probably doesn't want to join a company whose operations include meat-processing plants. Secondly, researching the company can reveal a lot about its stability. How long has the company been in existence? Has the company recently filed for bankruptcy? Is the company in the midst of battling one or more lawsuits, lawsuits that could shut down the company? You want to know the stability of the company, because you don't want to join it and then be out of a job two months or six months later.

As for what information you should research, here's a list to start with:

1. **When was the company started, and who were the founders?** To this day I am in awe of how critically important some interviewers consider this information. I have witnessed in multiple post-interview situations, after an interviewee indicated they knew nothing about the company, members of a hiring committee vehemently criticizing the candidate's lack of knowledge of the company's history. For many interviewers, not knowing the history of the company is insulting. Some interviewers will even consider the failure to do research on the company's history as an indication that the interviewee is not truly serious about the job. Is that really the impression you want to make? No, I am not saying that you need to know the names of the children and the pets of the founders. Yet, knowing who the founders were and the purpose of the company's founding are important facts to know. Likewise, knowing when the company started is important, because the year of its development and its years of existence help in understanding other facts regarding the company.

2. **Research the company's achievements.** Okay, this is where you could make some major bonus points in your interview. Being able to easily recall the company's

accomplishments will often show interviewers that you are energized about the prospect of working for them. It's also a way to understand where you would sit in the company's future and how you can best serve the company. Now, I'm not saying that you have to know every single achievement completed over a 50- or 100-year period. However, you should be able to identify 3 to 5 major accomplishments the company has achieved. I cannot stress enough the importance of identifying achievements relevant to the job that you are applying for. This is absolutely critical, because knowledge of such achievements will help you connect your skill sets that best match the position you're applying to and the company itself.

3. **Research the company's 5- and 10-year goals.** In my experience, knowing the short-term and long-term goals of the company is advantageous. During an interview, being able to tie in their goals with your achievements and skill sets is a great way to highlight just how well-suited you are for the position you're applying to. Now, when asked by an interviewer what you know about the company, being able to say "I understand you are trying to increase your market share in the next five years," can be a huge positive, because it shows you truly have done your research. But again, it is a major plus to be able to say "in my previous position as Marketing Director, I secured multiple million-dollar accounts that led to a $10increase in the company's market share." Statements like that are incredibly powerful, and will make it more likely you will be considered one of the top three candidates.

4. **Research the interviewers.** I myself went a little overboard on this one. After interviewing for one position, I shook hands with and thanked the members

of the interview committee. As one of the committee members had served in combat, I thanked him for his service. That comment certainly jolted him, after which he smiled and asked if I was part of the CIA. For the record, I got the job, but I also have never worked for the CIA. Yet, I think this shows you just how prepared I was for this interview. I knew the players, I knew the company's history, as well as the thorough history of the department I was applying to. Knowing the interviewers, their backgrounds, interests, and responsibilities, can help you gauge what type of questions those individuals are likely going to ask. In my last interview, I had asked who would be interviewing me and had been given a list of the hiring committee members. From there, it was simply a matter of tracking those individuals online and reviewing any and all biographies written on the company website about those individuals. You could take this a step further and research their LinkedIn profiles and any social media sites those individuals maintain. As a word of caution, professionals can receive a notice of who exactly has viewed their LinkedIn page. Now, if an interviewee researches my LinkedIn page, I take it as a sign that the individual is doing a thorough job in researching the situation. That is something I applaud. Some hiring managers or hiring committee members may take it as snooping (in other words they won't be happy). I for one research individuals through their LinkedIn and other sites, and I consider that just being thorough. I have no doubts there are others who make dummy LinkedIn accounts to hide their identity as they research people on LinkedIn. To interviewers and to interviewees, I say it is good thing to see a prospective employee researching all the players. You shouldn't take it as snooping when somebody, particularly an interviewee, reviews your LinkedIn page. Can't stress enough that somebody who's being thorough in their research will likely bring that same thoroughness to the job.

5. **Research contemporary industry concerns and developments.** Currently, colleges and universities throughout the world are struggling to reach their yearly admission goals, which means these institutions are generating less money every year. Add to that the fact that a large number of students never graduate from college. These students who are not "retained" negatively impact a college's or university's funds even further. Consequently, a priority in higher Ed at this time is in developing initiatives that increase student "retention" and graduation rates. For anyone applying for a job in higher Ed, bringing up ways you can help with retaining students or helping more students graduate can help you stand out from the crowd of applicants. Other industries have similar concerns and developments that periodically come up, and you must understand these major issues and find a way to bring them up in your interview. In so doing, you show hiring managers or hiring committee members that you are on top of industry standards and will likely be able to make a positive impact from day one of being given a job. Research your industry. As with the company's history and procedures, this is really something you should do before applying to a job. Actually, take this one step further and just maintain an understanding of ongoing developments in your field. That way you won't waste precious time doing such research right before your interview.

Research the Interview Site

Yes, I know I already mentioned this, but it is worth repeating that doing a test drive (or walk or bus ride) is critically important before the interview day. Personally, I get severely irritated when someone is late for a meeting (and even more so, a job interview). I have a lot to do each day of the week, whether it's serving as a college counselor during the day or working on my novels or writing résumés/cover letters/LinkedIn pages for clients in the evenings or on weekends. If I set up an appointment with someone, I have secured that space of time specifically for them. If the person arrives late, the rest of my day is usually impacted. Let me put this in another fashion. If you're late, I'm either going to have to cancel our meeting or going to have to cancel a meeting later on in the day. Why should I cancel an appointment for someone later in the day when it's your fault that my schedule is screwed up? Do you see what I'm getting at?

Now don't get me wrong, like most people, I understand that stuff happens and that people can be delayed because of weather, personal crises, traffic woes, or any of the unique circumstances that pop up now and again in all our lives. However, there are hiring managers and interview committee members who will not be as understanding, and if you're late for your interview (and even if the interview was rescheduled), you may already have ruined your chances of getting that job. Do you see why being on time is so important?

For this reason, taking time to plan out the drive and actually test driving the route to the interview site days in advance is important. I recommend that interviewees do a test drive at the same time of day they plan to travel to get to the interview. The importance of this is because you get to see the traffic patterns, whether it's a busy time a day with a lot of cars on the road or whether there's few people who will impact your commute.

Getting the lay of the land and investigating parking options and how to get into the building where the interview is being held are also important considerations. Take the time to do this, and you lessen the likelihood that you will be late for your interview. As a side note, I think that many interviewers will see your being late as a sign of things to come. That in a nutshell is why being on time is crucial when you're going to a job interview.

3

ACT AND DRESS THE PART

I'm a bit jaded here, because I have heard the phrase "dress for success" way too often in reference to a workshop that failed to deliver when it comes to what to wear to an interview. Now, that phrase regarding dressing for success is not a bad thing. It's just that there's so much more involved than just putting on a suit and a tie, wearing a pantsuit, or wearing a nice dress. The whole attitude you bring with you to the interview will help you make a positive or negative impact. You could be wearing a high-end suit that costs thousands of dollars, but it won't mean a damn thing if you walk in and are rude people in the front office area, such as secretaries or other office assistants. Now, I am well aware of the fact that there's a lot of professionals out there stating that job candidates need to be bold and take risks in order to stand out and make a lasting, positive impression. From my experience in all these years being a part of hiring initiatives, interviewees and interviewers take this advice to an extreme.

Let me be frank here. If you are interviewing for a position and walk in as if you own the place, treating support staff and even interviewers like you're a gift from God, a lot of the hiring committee members or hiring managers will rule you out as a possible candidate right from the start. By the way, just to reiterate something I mentioned earlier, a good interviewer is going to ask receptionists, secretaries, and other support staff how you treated them. An interviewee's interactions can tell you a lot about the person, good or bad. So, before we get into advisement about what to wear to an interview, here's a list of things you need to keep in mind as you are engaging in discussions with interviewers and other staff members at the business.

1. Be kind. This one's for you, Mom. My mom was the kindest person I've ever met. Heck, through my interactions with family and friends and my mom's colleagues, it was clear she was one of the nicest individuals most people had ever met. Forgive and forget... Be kind to all people... Help others whenever you can... My mom lived by these ideals and she instilled them into all of her children. Now, I have got a long way to go to live up to my mom's standards, but wherever I go and whomever I interact with, I remain ever-mindful of Mom's teachings. Having spent 11 years working in a restaurant, rarely did a day go by at work when I didn't see a customer treat a waitress, dishwasher, or cook as an inferior. In my profession far removed from the hospitality industry, I often seeprofessionals disrespecting service or support staff.treating support staff with the same manner of disrespect. For all of you reading this and everybody in the world, my mom does not approve! Regardless of whatever degrees you've earned or whatever achievements you have under your belt, you are no better than anyone else. Treat everyone you meet when you go to an interview with respect, dignity, and compassion. If you can't do this, why should anyone show you respect? Everyone you meet from parking attendants, to secretaries, and to other support staff should always be treated with kindness. If somebody is rude to you, move beyond the situation! Whether that person is just having a really bad day or she/he just happens to be a jerk doesn't really matter. Be kind and move on. If you reply to someone's rudeness with a curt response or disrespectful actions, you won't likely get the job.

Just a quick note here regarding dealing with rudeness: when you're being interviewed, whether it's by the interviewer or one of her/his support staff, you have the right to walk away. You have the right to say "I won't tolerate being treated like this." You most definitely want to do this in a respectful tone if you feel the need to leave an interview situation, but I am in no way advocating that you should sit and tolerate disrespect from anyone. When I was a young professional, there were times I interviewed for positions and support staff I encountered before the interview were less than pleasant. In those situations, I put on a smile and remained pleasant towards the individual. Maybe they were having a bad day, or maybe they just happen to be an unpleasant soul. Either way, who knew if I would ever see that person again?

Fortunately, I have never encountered an interviewer who was demeaning or disrespectful in any way, shape, or form. Now, you've got to make a decision in those situations. If unemployed, I still would not tolerate being treated disrespected by an interviewer, and I would excuse myself politely and leave. For someone who is unemployed who has dependents, walking away in an interview might be a harder thing to do. Consequently, this is a decision that each individual has to make on her/his own.

2. Be considerate. When you walk into a business for an interview, you need to remember that the people on staff have jobs to do. The process of interviewing applicants takes time, money, and the complex interweaving of departments to pull it off. So, when you show up at a receptionist's desk and he/she is on the phone, stand back away from the receptionist's desk and wait for him to finish his phone conversation and until he indicates you should approach. Remember, their job is not on hold while you interview. They have the same amount of work, except they now have to deal with the flood of applicants. That usually means they have less time in which to get their daily tasks done. Having an interviewee standing in front of them would be annoying and irritating. Don't be that interviewee! Give the support staff their space!

3. Engage in conversation. Now, it goes without saying that I struggle to engage with others. I mean, I truly hate speaking in public settings and would prefer to not have to attend any more meetings regardless of whether it was with a group of two people or a group of 20. A lifetime of battling an anxiety disorder will do that to someone! So, what the hell do I do when I get into an interview situation? I fight my anxiety and engage in conversation with people in the office. Your interaction is crucial to your success within an interview situation. Remember, the support staff you engage with before and after the interview will likely be included in the discussion as to whether you should be hired or not. For those twits, the intervieweeswho treat secretaries and receptionists as inferior beings, such blatant disrespect will be held against you! Consider it payback. With all this in mind, I strongly encourage you to start conversations with the support staff you encounter. Given my level of anxiety, I actually came up with a list of questions to ask support staff when I was waiting for my turn to have an interview. I am not talking about work-related questions, but instead I would ask support staff how their day was. Such general banter in conversations can show them that you would be a good colleague to work with. Furthermore, this interaction may provide some insights into what it's like to work in that business. You would be amazed at just what slips out when talking with someone. You may learn that there's a power grab going on at the office where two different partners are vying for ultimate control (this could mean the job you are applying to may not be as secure as they make it out to be). Other insights that could be gained from such conversations are that there are good or bad perks such as the supervisor either being understanding in letting staff leave for personal emergencies or a supervisor who is strict and doesn't allow for staff to easily deal with personal emergencies that pop up now and again. The bottom line is that you need to engage in conversation, or you will risk being seen as cold and distant. As an FYI, if you really can't think of anything to talk about, my go-to questions that I always put in reserve are to ask about any fish or plants on the secretary's desk... Just saying.

What to Wear

I am willing to bet that you have received a considerable amount of advice with regards to what to wear to a job interview. I'm sure most of what you have been told is decent with regards to appropriate dress for the interview. Let's just jump right in and get to the basics. In most settings, men should be wearing either a suit or nice pants with a dress shirt and sport coat. Yes, you should also be wearing a tie. Black, gray, or dark-blue suits are good options, whereas choosing a vibrant color such as purple or green may make you appear unprofessional to some interviewers. Why would I say that? Having served on interview committees, I have heard a lot of fellow committee members make less than charitable comments about interviewees who made **bold choices** with regards to the colors of their suits. Yes, there will be those who will see colors such as purple being the mark of an innovative, charismatic, and driven professional. Yeah, in most cases, not so much, at least from my experience. As you gain experience in your field, and you build a level of comfort engaging with colleagues within the region and you build a reputation, that would be more of the time to make bold choices. A more conservative approach to dress when you're first starting off in your career is in my opinion the better way to go. For women, a nice dress or pantsuit, again avoiding bold colors and patterns, is what I would recommend.

Now, for those of you who are working in industries where at the end of the day you go home and have to take a shower, your choice of clothes for an interview is usually much more relaxed. With two weeks shy of 11 years of experience as a cook and dishwasher and then with years of experience working as a professional field archaeologist, I can tell you that a more business-casual form of dress will likely be fine. Working in the service industries as a waiter, waitress, cook, or dishwasher, you should be fine with a nice pair of pants and maybe a polo shirt. For safety's sake, check with your colleagues as to what they would recommend for your particular field, especially any colleague who has served as a hiring manager. If you are uncomfortable with this level of casualness, go with a nice, button-down shirt and tie (no jacket). What about T-shirts? Avoid T-shirts at all costs! Especially T-shirts with political statements, vulgar language, or pictures of your favorite superhero. Yes, you may end up finding out that your boss encourages people to speak their mind politically or that he or she likes to see people wear Marvel T-shirts. However, for the interview, you should be more conservative in how you dress.

As for footwear, nice shoes are the way to go, at least in my opinion. There always seems to be somebody on the hiring committee that doesn't like to see an interviewee wearing sneakers. Admittedly, dress shoes can be ridiculously, and I mean really ridiculously, expensive. If you are strapped for cash, either purchase nice shoes from a discount store or get a pair from Goodwill. $15-$20 will get you decent shoes for interviews.

Backup Attire

Did I mention that I am riddled with anxiety? Let's just say that stuff happens on the way to interviews. What stuff? Everything from spilling coffee on your shirt and tie to stepping in a puddle that turns out to be a hidden lake. Yes, I am sure many will feel I am being overcautious, but I like to have backups, a lot of backups. What do I mean? I mean having backup socks, shoes, pants, shirts, and any accessories I may need for a job interview. In my own personal experience, I've only ever needed to change a shirt and tie because I spilled coffee on myself while driving to an interview. Again, when I have encountered an interviewee who clearly had suffered a wardrobe malfunction on the way to the interview, it hasn't bothered me in any way, shape, or form. However, other members of hiring committees I served on have not been so understanding.

As a side note, to hiring managers or hiring committee members who are so critical of an interviewee in such a circumstance, don't be such a twit!

I know that this sounds ridiculous, believe me I understand that. However, it is better to be safe than sorry. Do yourself a favor, and put a duffel bag with a change of clothes in your trunk. If you are taking public transportation to the interview, bring a bag with at least a change of shirt, tie, and pants with you. As I said, I only needed to use my backup clothes once in all these years, but I was damn glad to have those backups.

Jewelry

I am not going to spend pages and pages on this topic. Suffice to say, everyone should be wearing a watch to an interview. I understand that most people now rely on their cell phone to tell what time it is, but you should not have your cell phone out during the interview, because you will risk looking unprofessional and disrespectful. Having a watch allows you to keep track of time so that you know how much time there is remaining in your interview. Watch aside, lean towards the conservative side of things with regards to jewelry. Outrageously big earrings, bulky necklaces, or overly involved charm bracelets should be avoided. Why? They are a potential distraction to you and/or the interviewer. Just so you know, the clatter of charms from a charm bracelet against the countertop really drives some interviewers crazy. You have been forewarned.

If you wear a digital watch, make certain you turn off any alarms it is equipped with BEFORE the interview starts!!!

Bring a Notebook

Whatever position you are applying to, it is important to bring a notebook with you in addition to two slightly used pens. As for the pens, I mean two new pens that you used for the first time earlier that morning just long enough to get the ink flowing so the pens are ready to go right from the moment the interview starts. For those individuals, interviewees and interviewers alike, who show up without a pen or notebook to an interview, you will be seen by most of us as unprepared, unprofessional, and uninterested in the entire interview process if not the job itself. Yes, members of the hiring committees that don't bring a pen and notebook for recording notes look just as silly as interviewees who come unprepared to write notes down. Seriously, it's like the interviewer feels their presence alone is sufficient (you really look foolish).

As for the notebook, I recommend a pad folio with a fresh 8.5 by 11-inch legal pad in it. The reason I recommend that size is because if you are given any materials to take with you, you may come off as a little silly or unprofessional if you leave the interview room with a nice small pad filled with notes yet nothing to put handouts in. For those who prefer a smaller notebook, bring a two-pocket folder in which to place any documents you are given by the interviewer or hiring committee members.

4

HERE'S JOHNNY!!!!! MAKING YOUR ENTRANCE

Now, I know I'm going to upset a lot of people when I say the best entrance of anyone is when The Rock enters the building! Regardless of who you think has the best entrance, I think there's a little part in all of us that imagines a theme song playing when we enter a room for an interview, a theme that says, "Dammit, I am here!" When I prep clients for job interviews, I tell them to enter with confidence, which in many ways plays off this idea of a personal theme song. Fans of the *Ally McBeal* TV show probably know what I'm referring to. In any event, I am not suggesting that you have your cell phone play your theme song when you enter the room. In fact, please don't do anything of the sort. Instead, you need to focus on your entrance and how you interact in those first few minutes with an interviewer or members of a hiring committee if you truly want to have a chance at landing the job. If the first words out of your mouth are, "you can cancel all the other interviews, because I'm the best person for the job," I highly doubt anything you say beyond that point will be taken seriously. For the record, I have seen job applicants be similarly so recklessly bold, and those interviews ended quickly (no, they didn't get the job). So, what should you do when you are introduced, when you are standing before the interviewer or hiring committee for the first time? Here's a list of to-dos:

1. **Introduce yourself.** What, were you expecting something more profound? This moment in the interview is of tremendous importance. Before taking your seat, say something along the lines of, "good morning, I'm Neil O'Donnell, and it's a pleasure to meet you." If you've already met the interviewer, simply state it's good to see her/him again. If it's a hiring committee that you are meeting with, introduce yourself to each person, shaking each person's hand and greeting them accordingly. Do this before you sit down! Again, this may be me taking my parents advice to an extreme, but it is my recommendation.

2. **Use a firm handshake.** What, you thought we were joking about a firm handshake? No, the goal is not to break someone's hand. However, interviewers in my experience notice and remark on an interviewee's handshake if it's not firm. Petty that may be, it is something I have experienced where a member of a hiring committee commented on the weakness of the interviewee's handshake. Funny thing, a number of those who make snide comments about a weak handshake have themselves handshakes that are about as firm as a wet noodle. Yeah, just a little bit hypocritical. Frankly, I don't see how a handshake could in any way indicate how good a candidate is for the job. Unfortunately, there are self-righteous twits — I mean, interviewers and hiring committee members — who put a lot of stock in the firmness of a handshake. For that

reason, always keep a firm handshake. If you have to, practice your handshake with friends and family prior to an interview. Believe me, it will be well worth the investment in time.

3. **Make a record of the person's name.** Can you sense a bit of foreshadowing here? My mom instilled in us the need to thank people who helped us, whether it was a face-to-face 'thank you' or, preferably, a handwritten thank you note. Well, it's kind of hard to write a thank you note to someone if you don't remember their name. Now, as I stressed early on in this book, it will always help you to learn the names of the interviewers before the interview. That way you are simply putting names to faces as you go around the table and introduce yourself. As far as thank you notes, having the names ahead of time makes things so much easier as you can simply put a check next to the name of the person(s) who showed up. If you are not able to get that information ahead of time or if additional people showed up you weren't expecting at the interview, quickly and as surreptitiously as possible write their names down in the notebook I recommend that you bring to the interview. After the interview is over and you're back home, I recommend that you send typed letters or handwritten thank you notes to each person you interacted with, including the members of the hiring committee and the support staff you interacted with. We'll go over thank you notes later on.

4. **Thank you for giving me this opportunity.** This last bit of advice is my own personal recommendation, and is something that might not often be recommended or discussed. After sitting down and writing down the names as discussed, quickly look to everybody in attendance and simply thank them for the opportunity to

interview and state that you are excited for this opportunity. Why? In addition to being a polite thing to do, that initial breaking of the ice as it were is something that interviewers and interviewees struggle with. By getting the conversation rolling, you are helping out your interviewer tremendously.

5

SO MANY QUESTIONS

Cool, you're still here. Now we're getting to the part of interviews that really scare the living daylights out of interviewees: the questions themselves. Now, don't worry, I'm going to provide you with a list of good questions to prepare for and some insight on how to answer those classic questions effectively. Before that, let's discuss how you present yourself when responding to the questions you are asked.

1. **Look them in the eyes.** Seriously, eye contact is usually one of the first things discussed by hiring committee members the minute the candidate leaves the interview room. This is easier to do when you are being interviewed by one person. Yet, whether there is one interviewer or a committee of seven interviewers questioning you, maintaining eye contact with each person in the room is crucial to your success. Why? If you don't make eye contact with one or more of those interviewing you, an interviewer may take that as a sign of disrespect. Your answers to questions could be beyond perfect, and yet you will still not be considered

as a finalist for a position if you seemingly "disrespect" an interviewer for failing to make sufficient eye contact. So, how do you evenly spread eye contact amongst multiple interviewers? Great question. For every question you are asked, spend between 30-50% of your eye contact on the person who asked the question. The remaining eye contact time should be evenly distributed between the remaining members of the hiring committee.

2. **Be succinct in your answers.** Time is of the essence in most interviews, with many interviews only lasting an hour or less. Consequently, you want to thoroughly answer questions in as short a time as possible. Yes, you need to be detailed in your answers and make certain that you fully address the concerns of your interviewers. However, if you go off on tangents and tell stories to augment your responses, you'll find yourself running out of time and getting through very few questions. This is problematic, especially if interviewers don't get to ask the more important questions should they be saving those for the end of the interview time. When answering questions, it is a great idea to fit in to your answer's details and achievements from your work history that exemplify why you would be the best candidate for their consideration. For those questions that don't give you an opportunity to stress your skill and accomplishments relevant to the job you are applying to, be as brief as possible when providing answers. At the end of the interview, in the event that you think you did not give enough detail for a question asked early on in the interview, use time when they ask you if you've any questions to expand upon your earlier answers.

3. **Ask for clarification when needed.** To be sure, it is an uncomfortable situation when you're asked a question

and you don't really understand what the interviewer is asking you. However, we are all human, and an accomplished and skilled interviewer will be taking that fact into account. Interviewers understand that the interview process is stressful particularly when an applicant is sitting at a table facing two or more interviewers. Add to that the fact that some interviewers speak softly and are hard to hear, it is no wonder that interviewees stumble from time to time with understanding what's being asked. Just ask the interviewer to repeat the question or ask for clarification. A quick note for interviewers: be understanding when you're asking questions, because you've been in that seat yourself and know that it is really difficult to get through an interview. If an applicant or interviewee repeatedly needs a question restated and he or she still doesn't understand what you're asking, it might be a good sign that you need to look for another candidate.

4. **Don't be afraid to say you don't know.** None of us is all-knowing or perfect in any way. You are more than likely to be asked a question about a topic or about knowledge of a procedure or program that the company deems important for their hires to know. I am going to let you in on a little secret. It is usually quite clear when an interviewee is lying! If, for example, an interviewer asks you if you know how to use Microsoft Excel, and you have absolutely no clue how to use that program, be honest and tell them you don't know how to use it. If you say you do know how to use Excel when in fact you don't, within one or two more questions a good interviewer will get to the truth and realize that you just lied. I think for most interviewers catching a candidate lying is immediate grounds for dismissing that

candidate's application. On a quick note, if the job you are applying for requires you to have proficiency in a computer program or in some other form of skill and you don't have that skill, it is unlikely that you would be successful in that position. So, what is the best way to respond in such circumstances? Yes, admit that you don't know, but inform them that you are always willing to learn and always looking for ways to improve your performance and knowledge within the industry. Getting back to Excel, if you don't know how to use it but you are handy with computer programs, you should mention any similar programs you are experienced in, or just mention that you're good at learning new computer programs quickly. For the record, when I joined the HEOP program at Canisius College in 2003, I walked into an environment where most employees preferred to use Excel whereas I preferred Microsoft Access. Had I been asked if I knew Excel during my interview, I believe the best response would have been that while I was proficient in and preferred the use of MS Access, I was quite comfortable learning new database software and would seek out training to thoroughly understand Excel as soon as possible.

5. **Stay out of any infighting amongst the interviewers.** While rare in my experience, occasionally two or more members of a hiring committee get into a disagreement while they are interviewing a candidate for a job. Yes, such behavior during an interview is unprofessional at best. I would go further and say it is gross negligence on the part of those involved. In a few instances in my career, I as a member of the hiring committee needed to step in, diffuse a disagreement between hiring committee members, and get things back to the matter at hand — namely the interviewing of the candidate. As

interviewers, you should know better. As an interviewee, you need to be very careful here. True, most of these situations from my experience were simply two hiring committee members disagreeing about who is the best football, baseball, or basketball team. Such jovial disagreements are often lighthearted and lessen the tension in the room. However, even for such lighthearted disagreements, it's just better for an interviewee to not take sides. Frankly, in the event there is a full-blown argument that is far from lighthearted and centers on work procedures or anything else related to the job you're applying to, that should help you determine if that company is a good fit for you.

6. **Ask good questions.** What, you thought this was only about you answering questions? As they are asking questions to determine if you are a good fit for the position and the company, it is important for you to also determine if the position and the company are a good fit for you. Usually at the end of an interview, an interviewer or hiring committee members will offer the interviewee a chance to ask questions. We will discuss this further later on. Suffice to say, here you should be asking some questions. Better yet, if you have a chance to interact with hiring committee members before the commencement of the official interview, ask some basic questions to see if you can uncover what tasks the position you are applying for will entail. Doing so might just provide you with insight on how best to answer questions you will be asked during the interview. As for asking questions at the end of the interview, when they respond to your questions you should take that opportunity to clarify your skills and achievements that make you a good fit for the job.

7. **Be patient.** When responding to questions you are

asked, you may find one or more of the interviewers will struggle with asking questions. As a reminder, speaking in public is often difficult for the interviewers as well. Few professionals I have worked with enjoy the interview process, whether they are interviewing or they are being interviewed. So, asking a stranger questions can cause a bit of nervousness. In the event that an interviewer is struggling to get the words out but you know what they're trying to ask, it is a good idea trying to give them as much time as they need to get the question out. If you talk over them and say you know what they're asking, you will not only likely anger the interviewer, you will also likely upset other members of a hiring committee. As for the interviewer you interrupted? You very well could have just destroyed any chance of having a good relationship with them should you in fact be hired. For hiring committee members, such disrespect in the part of an interviewee is often too much to overcome. Be careful.

8. **Don't disparage or criticize others.** When a member of the hiring committee hears about past places you've worked, she may know some of the people you have likely worked with. In turn, the interviewer may ask you what you thought about the skills, temperament, or proficiency of a past supervisor or coworker. First of all, this interview is about you and only you. You should be respectful and not disparage or otherwise belittle anyone (no matter how incompetent or unprofessional a past colleague was). Doing so will at the very least portray you as a less than professional colleague or employee. Not the impression you ever want to make in an interview! Further, you will have no idea what type of connection the interviewer has with your previous employers or coworkers. You may be asked about a

previous employer's temperament in a way that suggests the hiring committee knows of the employer and does not respect the employer. Then, after you have made critical remarks about said employer, you'll go on to find that the committee members or member are actually good friends with the employer or colleague you just disparaged. Not only will you unlikely get the job, but if you're still working for that employer you just disparaged, you may end up losing the job you have. There's an added pitfall in such situations, when you're asked for your impression or thoughts on a previous colleague or a supervisor. Maybe the interviewer knows and despises your current or previous employer, and you respond to such questioning in a way that indicates you have little respect for that current or past employer. While you and the interviewer may clearly agree that the person you're discussing is inept and a jerk, it is likely that one or more members of a hiring committee, upon hearing your criticisms, may become very hesitant to hire you. Why? I think most people are hesitant to work with people who talk behind others' backs, which is essentially what you just did in mocking or disparaging a past employer or colleague.

9. **At the end, be respectful.** I can't help but be reminded of my mom and dad when I'm going through the interviewing process or when I'm coaching a client for a job interview. Politeness and showing respect were things my parents instilled in my siblings and me. At the end of the interview, show respect by again thanking an interviewer or hiring committee members for their time to both answer your questions and to give you an opportunity to interview for the job. Yes, I'm sure there are interviewers and/or hiring committee members who won't care either way whether you say thank you or not.

However, saying thank you for some interviewers is crucial for a job candidate to be considered for a job. Think about it. If you are hired, you will be representing the company when you interact with businesses, clients, and customers. If you do not show respect to an interviewer, the interviewer or hiring committee members may assume that you will be less than respectful and polite to others outside of the company. No good hiring manager is going to hire a candidate who is perceived as being rude or uncaring. Why else should you say thank you and shake hands again with each interviewer present? In the words of Mom and Dad, it's the right thing to do.

6

IMPORTANT INTERVIEW QUESTIONS TO PREPARE FOR

Well, you've made it through the entire book, and you reached what I consider to be arguably the most important section of this book. In this chapter, you will find a list of the questions that I've experienced as an interviewee and which I have asked as an interviewer. A number of these questions are very difficult to answer while some may seem par for the course and easy to manage. Regardless of the perceived difficulty level from your perspective, these are the questions that from my experience have been the most difficult and/or the most commonly asked questions in job interviews. Now, in addition to having my insights here, I urge you to talk to colleagues and professors within your respective field to gain their insights with regards to potential questions you may face and how to best answer them. Every industry is going to have its own quirks and its own nitpicking that will impact your answers to these questions. Because of this, having insight from the professors who trained you and colleagues that you trust is vital. Without further ado, here are the questions.

1. **Tell us a little about yourself?** This is certainly a

question fraught with danger, but it is also one of those questions that I feel is a great way to make an impact immediately on the hiring manager or hiring committee. Now once again, every hiring manager and committee member is going to have different levels of interest when it comes to asking questions and seeking answers. Having said that, I think it's safe to say that most interviewers are not looking for an interviewee to delve deeply into their hobbies when it comes to this question. Don't get me wrong, I think it can be helpful to bring up your interests, possibly a hobby, especially if you have won awards or other recognition locally, regionally, or nationally. From my experience, this information is secondary when it comes to this question. What a lot of interviewers want to hear is what it is about yourself that can be of great advantage for the company moving forward. Education, volunteers, statistic-backed achievements, and similar information are important to discuss at this time. Tell them what you have accomplished in this field thus far in your career. Remember the research portion of this book? Especially researching the company and the company's goals? Think to yourself, what experience and skills do I possess that will help the company reach those goals? As for the earlier-mentioned hobbies, get a feel of the room before you mention hobbies or interests outside of your profession. In some circumstances, you will find the interviewers are very relaxed and quite humorous to be honest. Such interviewers will get a kick out of knowing that you like to kayak even though you almost went over Niagara Falls. Other interviewers, however, are rather cold and seeking only to know how you can contribute to the company and/or the department. As for the statistic-backed achievements I mentioned, if for example you are applying to a sales department, being able to say that you were directly responsible for a 10% increase in sales at your last employer has more weight than saying, "I'm good at sales," or "I'm really good at sales."

2. **What do you know about our company?** This is absolutely, positively, one of my favorite questions all-time! And from all the hiring committees I've been a part of, this is often the question that senior managers and program directors use to rule out candidates. When I advised you earlier to research about the company, part of my reasoning behind advising that step was to prepare you for this very question. You need to know the history of the company, and you had better learn of its major accomplishments and short-term and long-term goals. Why? Because if you don't, the interviewer or interviewers may rule you out as a good candidate arguing that you didn't take the time to learn about the company you were trying to join. Many interviewers see this as a sign of disrespect. Frankly, with access to the World Wide Web and so many companies having websites, Facebook pages, and Twitter feeds, there is no excuse for not being able to learn about the company before your interview. When you apply to the job, there were probably at least another hundred people who also applied. Many if not most of these individuals sent in generic résumés and generic cover letters, which stand out like a sore thumb. Such candidates are often seen as not serious and will likely not get an interview. If you can't answer this question, providing good details about the company you're applying to, you'll likely be instantly placed in the category of not serious candidates. I cannot stress this enough. Do your research and know

the company's focus, history, accomplishments, and goals.

3. **Where do you see yourself in five years?** This is another good question. Let me remind you, the hiring process cost significant amounts of time and money. Equally important, most employers and staff don't enjoy the hiring process, so they won't be thrilled if the interviewee says in five years he or she wants to be owning their own business. A company and its employees don't want to be going through the same process in five years. They are more than likely looking for somebody who's going to put in more than 3 to 5 years, preferably 10 years. Sure, if you're fresh out of high school or college, anyone interviewing you is likely going to realize that in 3 to 5 years you'll be looking for a new job. However, to come out in the interview and say that is a big mistake. When asked this question, I recommend that you answer in a way that you see yourself helping the company achieve its goals (you know the goals because you researched them). To make a greater impact, discuss how your particular skill sets will be helping you to move the company forward to reach goals. Then, refer back to your work history and discuss achievements you made that back up the fact that you can obtain those goals. Being specific here with regards to statistics detailing your achievements would be helpful. A good response would be "if hired, I plan to be using my experience securing million-dollar accounts to help your company increase it's market share and customer retention rates by at least 10%."

4. **If you could have any superpower, what would it be and why that superpower?** There always seems to be that one interviewer that asks weird questions. I mean, really weird questions. To be honest, I've actually seen

lists of "recommended" questions on "best of" lists in
publications and on the internet. On those lists, I often
see the "superpower" question. Now, for answering, it's
hard at times to know the mindset and style of humor
your interviewers possess. Some just use such questions
to lighten the mood during a stressful situation. Other
interviewers, meanwhile, are looking for answers, even
to such weird questions, that show why you would be
the best candidate. I recommend you consider splitting
the difference. What do I mean? Answer with a
superpower that would provide you with a great skillset
for you work, something that would make you more
effective, and then add a secondary superpower that is
just for fun. For example, as a professional counselor, I
would love the superpower to read thoughts to know
what was truly bothering my clients, what questions
they had but were too afraid to ask. I could then add,
"from a fun standpoint, I would love to be able to fly so
I could make it back and forth to conferences without
having to deal with airports." The second superpower
was more of something for fun, but I still replied in a
way that the superpower would make me more effective
at work (by using the ability to fly to attend
opportunities to build my counseling skillsets through
conference lectures and workshops).

5. **If you had ten million dollars, how would you spend
your time?** This is another of those weird questions that
pops up from time to time. Once again, I suggest you
answer in a way that would show your connection to the
job you are applying for. Stating that you would retire
may be what you would likely do, but I encourage a
different viewpoint. In your mind, change the question
to, "if you had ten million dollars, what are things you
would do to strengthen your professional skills."

Traveling to see "best practices" in other countries (for the field you are in) is certainly one way to go. Another good answer would be to consider any community service you would do should you receive a ton of money. Also, stating a wish to pursue continued education (master's degree, bachelor's degree, or some certificate program relevant to your field) would be a good response as far as I am concerned.

6. **How would you handle and argument with a coworker?** Arguments happen quite a bit in the workplace and are something employers hate dealing with. So, to prevent their possibly hiring a new staff member with anger management issues, hiring managers and committees are often asked to ask applicants about how a job candidate handles arguments with coworkers. From my conversations with employers as well as my workplace observations, employers prefer staff handle disagreements "professionally" without bothering the boss or other superiors, actions which often then require mountains of paperwork and a costly investigation by HR. If asked this question, a good response would be that you would speak with the colleague to work things out and to see how you may have contributed to the argument. From there, indicate your hope to come to an agreement with the colleague and build a better rapport with her/him.

7. **How would you handle a disagreement with a supervisor?** Yeah, now is definitely NOT the time to joke by saying something like "push him out a window." Seriously, this is a question I don't believe leaves room for kidding. How do I handle such disagreements and how would I answer this question? Simply put, I would ask my supervisor if we could meet to discuss the situation. From there, I would ask the

supervisor how they would like me to handle the situation (the cause of the disagreement) in the future. I would explain my perspective if given an opportunity, and I would make certain to check in with the supervisor on a regular basis moving forward to update her so we were always on the same page (less likely then that disagreements would occur in the future). I would also evaluate my role in the disagreement and apologize as warranted.

8. **Are you comfortable working as part of a team?** Teamwork, in most work environments, is essential for increasing operational efficiency while working with ever-shrinking budgets. In other words, you need to be comfortable working as part of a team. Teamwork is inevitable, so you best get comfortable with it. If asked this question, I would also put in that in addition to your enjoying collaborating with colleagues, that you also are ready to take initiative as circumstances dictate. For many employers, such self-motivators are highly sought after. Again, give examples of how you effectively worked as part of a team in the past within work settings.

9. **What are ways you keep current on best practices and new theories or technologies in the field?** I don't care how many degrees or certificates you have, there is always something new to learn, and employers usually like to hire professionals who understand the importance of continuing their education. Beyond changes in technology (particularly computer software/programming), most fields are continually evolving with new methodologies and theories (also known as new "best practices"). From the technology standpoint, you should definitely be keeping up to date on tech changes relevant to your field and inform

interviewers of continuing education units (CEUs) that you have recently acquired (yes, you should be seeking additional training at all times). Don't know where to find opportunities to get CEUs in your field? Type your field and "ceu" into any search engine. From there, find CEUs that are provided by 'Accredited' organizations. You might even want to ask the interviewer if the company provides support for attending conferences or completing CEUs. Yes, many employers will help employees pay for continuing their education. As a last bit of advice with this question, I recommend that you look online for free CEUs immediately and complete one or more so that you can inform interviewers of recent examples of continuing education that you have successfully completed.

10. **Why should we choose you?** Telling an interviewer, "because I'm the best," generally won't cut it. In fact, such a response will probably sink your candidacy immediately. Consider being humble in this moment, if asked this question, and make sure to reiterate your skills and achievements that match the job ad/job description of the job you are applying for. "I am sure you are interviewing many capable candidates. I believe what makes me a standout is my years of experience related to the job and the specific successes I have made accordingly." Give specific experience and achievement examples from your work history that align with what skills the interviewer has identified as of critical importance in the job ad AND during the interview.

11. **What is your biggest weakness?** We all have weaknesses, so I don't advise answering this question by saying, "I have no weaknesses." I have a hard time taking any candidate seriously if they say that in response. In other words, be honest and forthright. What

I recommend is that you consider mentioning a weakness that you have already made an effort to work on (though not a weakness connected to one of the main skills that the interviewer identified as crucial to the position you are applying to). For an example, I have said indicated in interviews that "public speaking" has been a weakness of mine. I then follow that up immediately by saying than I have been making a greater effort to voice my ideas, questions, or concerns during staff meetings AND I have likewise sought out opportunities to present at conferences, board meetings, staff meetings, or other public events/venues.

12. **What was your biggest career mistake?** This question is certainly akin to the one about your "biggest weakness." Again, no one is perfect, and we all have made mistakes in our careers, mistakes big and small. Be honest about having made mistakes, but again, pick a mistake that is minor with regards to the position you've applied to and discuss how you learned from the experience and have made corrections. Let's get back to my "public speaking" weakness. A mistake I could mention is having struggled to provide a clear update during a meeting with my boss because of my difficulty with public speaking. After the meeting with my boss, I sent a follow-up memo/email addressing questions I could not answer at the time of the meeting. I also worked hard on developing my public speaking skills, even presenting at a regional conference, and as a result, I am now more confident, clear, and concise when presenting in staff meetings.

13. **How did your previous job help prepare you for this one?** Any job listed on your resume is fair game for an interviewer, and make no mistake, many interviewers want to know how your past work qualifies you for the

job you are applying to. For that reason, be sure you are ready to explain why each job you listed on your resume prepared you for success at the job you are hoping to be hired for. How did a past job train or prepare you for specific tasks listed in the job description for the job you are applying for? Make sure you can provide details.

14. **What would you like us to know about you or what question do you wish we had asked you?** I find this question causes interviewees a lot of stress. Go to the interview prepared to answer this question! Now, some may think this a good point to let your personality shine through, and I would agree to an extent. Maybe let them know you travel or do a lot of hiking or even that you do a lot of community service. Those would usually be acceptable responses. There is another approach to consider though, at least as far as I am concerned. Use such a question as an opportunity to further explore your strengths and experience connected to the position. For instance, if you were applying for a marketing position, letting them know in your spare time that you volunteer at a local non-profit organization providing marketing support would both show your dedication to community service and your efforts to further develop and enhance your marketing skills. Take every opportunity through interview questions to reiterate your skills and experience that make you a good fit for the job.

15. **Do you have any questions for us?** There is only one wrong answer to this question as far as I am concerned: "NO." Don't pass up a chance to ask questions. I for one have never been comfortable in interviews asking for clarification on salary and benefits (I usually leave that to interviews in the later stage of the process). As with previous questions, try to ask questions in a way that

you can reiterate your relevant skills and experience. Using the marketing professional example from the last question, let me demonstrate. If given a chance to ask a question, a good question to consider would be the following:

"Currently I have been seeking and completing continuing education opportunities to gain new marketing skills by attending conferences and company-sponsored marketing workshops. Does your company provide time and support for the pursuit of continuing education/ongoing training related to our positions?"

With that question, I let the interviewer know I will keep learning new skills and enhancing my marketing toolkit; that's something employers generally love to see. It also reiterates again that I am a marketing specialist through experience AND training. Such a question can leave a good impression while also letting you know if the company pays for attendance to conferences (which could be a huge benefit). With any question, try to reiterate your skills, experience or training that tie into the job you are applying for. **ASK AT LEAST ONE QUESTION!**

7

CONCLUDING REMARKS

Nope! You are not done yet. After the interview ends, I have asked interviewers what is the timeline for when decisions would be made. Some feel this is a rude thing to ask, something that might irritate a hiring manager or committee member. Most of the hiring committee members I've served with did not have any issues with an interviewee asking that question. For one of my jobs, it was nearly a year before I heard anything (I in fact got the job); I wish I had asked what the timeline was for the decision, because I would have been seeking other opportunities (part-time) to gain experience and generate savings. I would suggest you ask the head of the hiring committee or the department head if you will also have a meeting with your potential future boss after getting grilled by the hiring committee. Why? Members of a hiring committee usually have no idea when final decisions will be made whereas the person in charge likely would.

As for saying your goodbyes, you should consider handing out personal business cards and ask the hiring committee members or other interviewers to please contact you should they have any additional questions. No, you should not be handing out your business card from the current employer you work for; that is unprofessional, and you should not be using your current work resources (email, phone, etc.) for applying for new jobs. Have your own personal cards made that include your permanent address, your personal phone number (cell preferably), and a personal email address (preferably Gmail account as AOL and Hotmail accounts are often considered "old school" or otherwise outdated).

Just an FYI: I use my Hotmail account for everything not related to my job, because I love Hotmail; I almost never use my Gmail account. That said, I have heard hiring committee members make less than charitable comments about AOL and Hotmail, which is why I recommend a Gmail account. As for hiring committee members and hiring managers who think AOL and/or Hotmail are outdated and lacking professionalism, you're being a twit. Both should be acceptable.

Continuing with the business card, I recommend you also include any website or social media site you manage that is related to your profession. Hand the cards out to anyone who interviewed you. Then, on your way out, say thank you and goodbye to those you interacted with but who were not in the interview asking questions (i.e., the secretary or receptionist).

Go Unwind

After leaving an interview, I recommend you take time to decompress and relax. Take yourself out for a coffee or lunch. Give yourself time to release the stress you endured during the interview process. It is usually a good idea to update a mentor or colleague of yours who knew about the interview. After letting them know of the interview's completion, you can run by them any concerns or questions you have to try and assess your performance. Be careful here; don't stress too much about what you potentially did right and wrong. Sometimes jobseekers get so worked up because they forgot to mention something in the interview that they stop back at the company or call their interviewer(s) directly to see about scheduling a meeting to further discuss their skills. I find a lot of hiring managers/committees are not fond of this. Just go and relax, because there are other ways to correct such oversights, ways which I feel are more professional and effective (see advice on thank you notes).

Thank You Notes

I know, shocker! I'm bringing up saying thank you again. Thank you notes will be expected by some interviewers and/or hiring committee members. Some, frankly, don't care — or worse, they see it as a job applicant trying to 'suck up' to the committee. It's really a mixed bag when it comes to reactions to thank you notes (and how thank you notes should be done). Here are my tips regarding thank you notes:

1. **Send thank you notes.** From my experience on hiring committees, many interviewers expect to receive thank you notes from interviewees after the interview. I have never heard a committee member say they didn't want to receive a thank you note, but I have heard multiple committee members over the years comment in a negative tone how they were unhappy about the fact that an interviewee did not send a thank you note. Play it safe and send a thank you in my opinion. More importantly, sending a thank you is what Mom and Dad consider to be a necessity out of respect.

2. **Typed instead of handwritten.** If you have gorgeous, easy to read handwriting, then by all means handwrite your thank you note, whether you use generic thank you

cards or you write a letter. Handwritten notes can make a great impression! However, as most handwritten messages and thank you notes I have received are hard to read and understand, I recommend typing the thank you and then including a handwritten signature. While you are at it, use a font that is easy to read (if the thank you recipient can't read your note or letter, it is not going to be very effective in conveying your gratitude).

3. **Send notes to all interviewers.** Whether you were interviewed by one person or a committee, you should attempt to send a thank you note to everyone who interviewed you. Remember the earlier discussion of writing down names of your interviewers? Here's where that list comes in handy. After going to the company website to track down an interviewer's contact information, send them a thank you note. If you have forgotten the name of one or more of the interviewers, you have a couple options. First, you can simply send one thank you to the head of the hiring committee and say you are grateful to all the hiring committee members. A second option would be to call the secretary for the company and ask for the names and addresses of your interviewers.

4. **Send thank you notes to support staff you interacted with.** If you were aided by a secretary or receptionist and you spoke with that individual for any length of time, it might be worth it to send her or him a thank you note, even if it is just to say you appreciate their assistance and it helped you relax and better understand the company and department.

5. **Send the notes quickly.** You should be sending out thank you cards or letters between 24 to 48 hours after the interview (I always try to have the thank you notes out in 24 hours. The longer you delay sending a thank

you, the less likely it will help your candidacy, at least from my experience.

6. **Make the thank you impactful!** Don't just write that you are thankful for their interviewing you! Mention specific things from the interview, such as you are thankful for the interviewer providing insight into the company's history or future goals. Additionally, a thank you letter or card provides a good opportunity to reinforce your interview: restate your interest in the position and your skills that you feel make you a good candidate for the position. As for the aforementioned stress regarding your wish to clarify a statement you made, use the thank you note to accomplish that.

Check in; Don't Stalk.

As stated earlier, it is a good idea to ask at the interview's end about the timeline for when decisions would be made. A week to ten days after the date indicated as when decisions would be made is the earliest I would consider calling to check on the status of your application. Honestly, I wait until called and move on to other things. I try not to stress about things I can't control. On the flipside are those who check in a minimum of once per week regarding a decision on their candidacy. These individuals could (and sometimes do) wear out their welcome, causing their candidacy to be no longer considered. Be patient.

Conclusion

There you have it! My advisement for tackling job interviews. It gets easier over time, but until then, this advice is what I provide students and clients, most of whom do extremely well in interviews after employing the aforementioned strategies. One last piece of advice is for you to practice answering questions

BEFORE an actual interview. Have a colleague grill you on questions, or go to your college's career center or alumni department and request assistance in preparing for job interviews. Many colleges and universities do provide such support. This is your career, so put the effort in and you should see real progress early on. In the event an interview does not go well, dust yourself off and move on. Even bad interviews provide valuable experience! Keep at it, and you will break through the interview barrier. Just be patient.

Dear reader,

We hope you enjoyed reading *Job Interview Essentials*. Please take a moment to leave a review, even if it's a short one. Your opinion is important to us.

Discover more books by Neil O'Donnell at https://www.nextchapter.pub/authors/neil-odonnell

Want to know when one of our books is free or discounted? Join the newsletter at http://eepurl.com/bqqB3H

Best regards,
Neil O'Donnell and the Next Chapter Team

Job Interview Essentials
ISBN: 978-4-86745-939-3

Published by
Next Chapter
1-60-20 Minami-Otsuka
170-0005 Toshima-Ku, Tokyo
+818035793528

18th April 2021

CPSIA information can be obtained
at www.ICGtesting.com
Printed in the USA
BVHW081809040521
606416BV00005B/571

9 784867 459393